FLORIDA

Past and Present

Sarah Sawyer

rosen publishing's
rosen central

New York

Dedicated to Marshal Devine

Published in 2010 by The Rosen Publishing Group, Inc.
29 East 21st Street, New York, NY 10010

Library of Congress Cataloging-in-Publication Data

Sawyer, Sarah.
Florida: past and present / Sarah Sawyer.—1st ed.
    p. cm.—(The United States: past and present)
Includes bibliographical references and index.
ISBN-13: 978-1-4358-5288-4 (library binding)
ISBN-13: 978-1-4358-5574-8 (pbk)
ISBN-13: 978-1-4358-5575-5 (6 pack)
1. Florida—Juvenile literature. I. Title.
F311.3.S25 2010
975.9—dc22

                                                                    2008054223

Manufactured in the United States of America

CPSIA Compliance Information: Batch #CR014001YA: For Further Information Contact Rosen Publishing, New York, New York at 1-800-237-9932

On the cover: Top left: Fort Matanzas on Florida's Rattlesnake Island. Top right: The harvesting of Florida's Valencia oranges in Immokalee. Bottom: The Kennedy Space Center in Cape Canaveral.

Contents

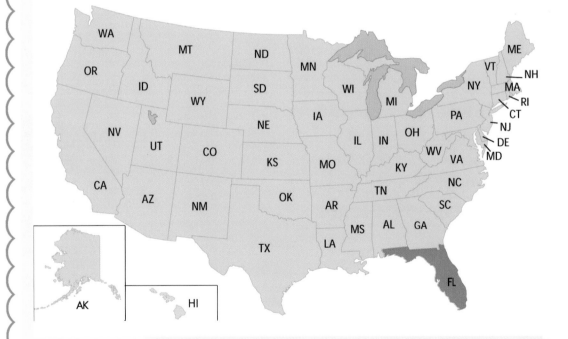

Florida is a peninsula, which means that it is bordered by water on three sides. This southern state boasts amazing land and water features, as well as a rich and diverse cultural history.

Introduction

As far back as twelve thousand years ago, the land we now know as Florida was home to such majestic creatures as the mastodon, the giant armadillo, and the saber-toothed tiger. Over the millennia, as people inhabited the land, they learned to hunt, farm, build tools, and trade goods and services with nearby communities.

Today, the people living in Florida don't just trade with each other. People come from all over the world to visit Florida. When they do, they stay in hotels, eat in restaurants, and visit amusement parks, museums, beaches, and other entertainment spots. Tourism and international trade are Florida's biggest businesses, but there are more. Exciting industries like space travel are also big business in the state.

Florida is a unique place. There's no state that's quite like it. From its unique geographical characteristics to its intricate culture and history, there is a lot to know, and love, about Florida.

Maybe you live in Florida. Maybe your family has a Florida vacation planned and you want to learn more about the place you'll be visiting. Perhaps you'd just like to know more about a great state with an amazing history and lots of great stories. Any, and all, of these reasons are great ones to pick up this book. As you work your way though these chapters, you'll not only learn about the way Florida used to be, but also about what Florida is like today.

THE LAND OF FLORIDA

Florida is unlike any other state in America. One of the main reasons is that its land is unlike any other state. Florida is a peninsula. This means that on three sides, Florida borders water. That's special. This creates lots of beaches and oceanside communities. The beaches bring sunbathers, but there is also the risk of flooding, hurricanes, and other weather events. To understand the state, you first have to understand the land.

Long ago, almost twelve thousand years ago, Florida wasn't part of any country. There was just land and wilderness, and it was very different from how it looks now. The water level was much lower. Land that is now at the sea bottom was then dry and quite unlike what the land is today. Where there are now rivers and lakes, there was dry land with small bubbling springs. Florida did not have the wetlands and swamps it does today. Rather, it looked much more like a prairie or a desert. It did not have palm trees and citrus fruit; instead, it had pine forests and prairies filled with tall grasses.

The climate was different, too. During this time, Florida experienced more dramatic changes of seasons. Today, it is generally warm and sunny in Florida year-round. But thousands of years ago, it had cold winters and hot summers in much the same way that more northern states experience seasons today.

The Florida Keys have become highly developed in the past fifty years. This is how the land looks now, but there was a time when the state was much more rural.

The people who lived on the land that is now called Florida are often referred to as Paleo-Indians. Scientists have found some tools, bones, and other artifacts deep in the ground that lead them to believe that these people lived in very simple societies in which they hunted, gathered plants, and traded with other nearby groups of people. Scientists have also found carved wooden stakes that were probably used to hold up tent-like shelters.

As the land and weather changed, so did the people living on the land. They developed more complex societies. Later, around the year 250 CE, the people living in Florida were organized enough to work

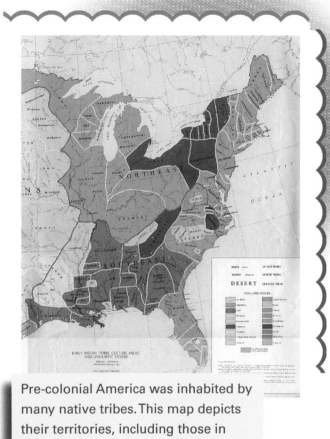

Pre-colonial America was inhabited by many native tribes. This map depicts their territories, including those in Florida.

together, digging with wooden and shell tools, to build a system of canals they could use to travel from their well-developed city to the ocean. Robert Carr, executive director of Archaeological and Historical Conservancy in Davie, Florida, said of this recent discovery in the *New York Times*, "In adapting to their wetland world, the people of South Florida achieved a level of cultural sophistication and social organization much earlier than previously believed." As far as we know, these were the first canals built to make travel easier and faster. For almost twelve thousand years, tribes like the Timucua, Tocobaga, Calusa, Apalachee, Mayaca, Hororo, Utina, Saturiwas, Potano, Mocoso, Pohoy, and Ais lived, worked, and built societies in Florida.

Florida's Land Today

Of course, Florida is not a desert anymore. Today, there are not only lakes and rivers but also towering cities, remote wetlands, and lush tropical forests. Most of Florida can claim to get as much as 50 inches

(127 centimeters) of rain a year. Fortunately, it doesn't all come at once. A quick look at Florida's climate patterns reveals that one year there may be flooding and the next there may be drought. This has a significant effect on both agriculture and tourism, which are Florida's biggest businesses.

Florida is one of the fastest-growing states, surpassed by only California and Texas. Some of the immigrants to the state come from places like Mexico, Puerto Rico, Costa Rica, Guatemala, Honduras, Nicaragua, Panama, El Salvador, Argentina, Bolivia, Chile, Colombia, Ecuador, Paraguay, Uruguay, and Venezuela. They come from a diverse array of cultures and speak many different languages and dialects.

One of Florida's most amazing immigration stories is that of the Cuban American people. According to Dario Moreno, associate professor of political science at Florida International University, "of the 833,120 Cubans who live in the Sunshine State, a remarkable 650,601 reside in Miami-Dade County. In other words, over half of all Cubans in the United States [52 percent]

Costumed dancers perform in a parade through Little Havana during Calle Ocho, one of Miami's celebrations of Cuban culture.

9

Florida's Land

Florida used to be larger than it is now. It also used to be colder. Global climate changes caused polar waters to melt, which made the sea level rise and caused the flooding of Florida's coasts. As a result, the part of Florida's landmass that rises above sea level is smaller today than it was in ancient times.

Many factors can lead to climate change. Today, we can see that climate change may result in further changes to Florida's landmass. Sea levels are expected to rise between 8 and 30 inches (20.32 and 76.2 cm) by 2100, according to the Natural Resources Defense Council. There are things people can do to help. Using less electricity, walking or biking instead of driving, and generally supporting clean energy whenever possible can help prevent these changes.

and over three-fourths [78 percent] of all Cubans in Florida live in just one county." The Cuban population affects politics, architecture, food, music, art, and everything else that happens in this part of Florida; they are part of what makes the people in Florida so very interesting. Another factor, of course, is the water.

The Water's Effect on the Land

Water has a lot to do with the land and climate of Florida. Nowhere is this clearer than in the beautiful Everglades. The Everglades is a network of ponds, prairie, and forested uplands that at one time covered almost 11,000 square miles (28,600 square kilometers) in southern Florida. It is often referred to as "the river of grass" because it is long and winding like a river, but it is different from most rivers. More marsh or

Florida's wetlands are home to birds, fish, and other animals found in few other parts of the country. The great white egret is just one of the many exotic species there.

swamp than actual river, the water is less than 10 inches (25.4 cm) deep in some places and as wide as 60 miles (97 km) in others.

The southern fifth of the Everglades has been designated a national park, which means its land and wildlife are protected by law and supported with government funds. This is an important way to protect the unique combinations of plants and animals that make up the Everglades' ecosystem.

Chapter 2

THE HISTORY OF FLORIDA

People often say Ponce de León "discovered" Florida. That's not true. People lived there for thousands of years before he traveled the ocean. Ponce de León was just the first European explorer to land in what we now call Florida in 1513.

Ponce de León came to Florida twice, once in 1513 and again in 1521. He, like many European explorers of his time, came to "claim" land, gold, silver, and other natural resources for his wealthy patrons back home. The fact that he made the journey twice is amazing. Back then, travel was not as easy as it is today. The voyage from Spain to Florida by sea was long and hard. Many of the people who came with Ponce de León did not survive the journey. Many of those who did survive did not live long after they arrived in Florida. There were natives already there, and they did not want to relinquish their land. The first group of European immigrants that came with him met with violence from the people already living there. Therefore, colonization was not easy.

In 1539, Hernando de Soto also ventured to Florida in search of riches for his patrons. His approach differed from Ponce de León's in that he was less interested in colonizing the land and more interested in stealing the wealth he thought the native people had hidden away. He wandered the land for many years with a small band of explorers. He died of a fever, but his band of explorers traveled on to Mexico to continue exploring.

The French were as interested as the Spanish when it came to colonizing Florida. Jean Ribault and René Goulaine de Laudonnière—both French explorers— came to what is now Jacksonville and set-tled in the area.

The Spaniard Pedro Menéndez de Avilés came in 1565. He was determined to run the

In 1513, the Spanish conquistador Ponce de León traveled to Florida's shores in search of gold, silver and the fabled fountain of youth.

French out of the area. We now refer to the area he settled as St. Augustine. This was the first of many lasting settlements in Florida, but it was not a smooth transition. Many countries wanted to settle the area, and they were willing to fight each other for the right to do so. There were many battles, wars, and skirmishes fought between people who would settle and between the settlers and the native peoples already living there.

The British established nearby colonies and fought with Spain for control of the area. They experienced some success. During the American Revolutionary War, both East and West Florida chose to

The European explorer who came to settle St. Augustine in the 1500s created one of the earliest and longest-lasting settlements.

stay in contact with England, even as other colonies fought for independence. British control didn't last long, though. A few years after the battle of Pensacola in 1781, the Spanish regained control of Florida, and Spanish settlers flooded in. Americans who preferred the Spanish laws and systems of government to those in the new America moved to the territory. Africans who were living in slavery in nearby states also fled to Florida, where they had some hope of escaping the system of slavery.

While Florida was Spanish by law, it was culturally becoming more and more American, and the U.S. government wanted to

Native Americans in Florida

There were many native tribes in Florida at one time, and there are still Native Americans of many traditions to be found there, but not in the numbers there once were. Only a fraction of the native population that once lived in Florida lives there now.

However, as time progresses, some groups are banding together to celebrate their heritage and enjoy a stronger presence than they have in previous years. The Seminole are one such example. Many Seminole had been killed after the Seminole Wars at the end of the 1800s. Those left were living in poverty and hiding in camps they built in the wetland swamps and marshes of southern Florida. Eventually, the political climate changed and people no longer had to hide in the swamps. They moved to reservations or to cities. In the future, the tribe hopes to find ways to live fully connected to their ancient culture while also working in the same mainstream economy as other Floridians. They hope to remain connected both to modern society and to their ancient traditions. We all stand to benefit if they do.

include it in its territory. The U.S. government made official (and unofficial) military overtures toward Florida. And Spain, realizing it would not be able to hold out much longer, eventually turned the territory over to the United States. Florida officially became a U.S. territory.

Statehood and the Civil War

On March 3, 1845, Florida became the twenty-seventh state to join the United States of America. The wars between the U.S.

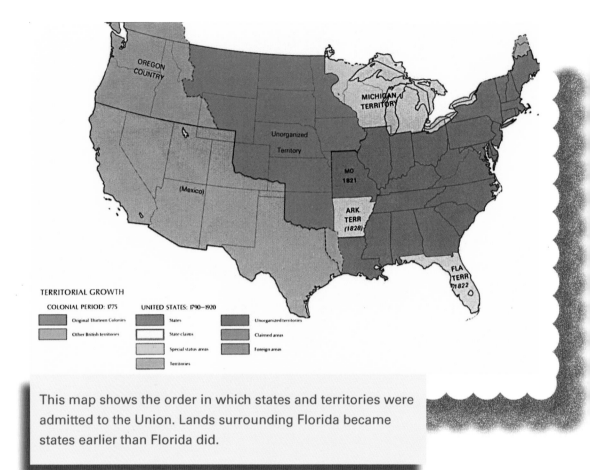

TERRITORIAL GROWTH

COLONIAL PERIOD: 1775

Original Thirteen Colonies

Other British territories

UNITED STATES: 1790–1920

States

State claims

Special status areas

Territories

Unorganized territories

Claimed areas

Foreign areas

This map shows the order in which states and territories were admitted to the Union. Lands surrounding Florida became states earlier than Florida did.

government and those living in Florida ended, but a new kind of war was starting. When Florida joined the country, it joined in the problems the country was having, such as the impending Civil War.

Very shortly after Abraham Lincoln was elected president of the United States, Florida sided with others in the Confederate States of America. Some Floridians fought for the North and some for the South. While there was great loss in Florida, there was not quite the devastating destruction that was experienced in other Confederate states.

Rebuilding the South called for lumber and other supplies. Florida was able to provide these resources. This was the beginning of development and industry in Florida. As others began to depend on things grown in, made in, or shipped to Florida, businesses grew and industry developed. It was this spirit of development that brought Florida into the Industrial Revolution.

Chapter 3

THE GOVERNMENT OF FLORIDA

Since Florida became the twenty-seventh state to join the United States of America, it has had a rich political history. Just like other states, Florida has a state government system that is divided into three branches: executive, legislative, and judicial. Similar to the federal government, these branches of state government work both independently and interdependently. They work in their own area of expertise, but they keep each other in check. We call this the system of checks and balances. This system helps ensure that no one section of government has too much power.

Executive Branch

The executive branch of Florida's government is most concerned with administering and enforcing laws. The governor is the head of this part of the state government and is the chief law enforcement officer. The governor is supported by a lieutenant governor and a cabinet of supporting politicians: an attorney general, a chief financial officer, and a commissioner of agriculture. Together, the cabinet has power that is equal to the governor. This helps spread the power and make sure that these people work together to make the best decisions possible for the state.

Charlie Crist, the forty-fourth governor of Florida, has worked on many issues, including identity theft and civil rights.

Voting Complications

In 2000, the very close presidential election was complicated by what has come to be known as Florida's "hanging chad debacle." Votes cast there were mismarked and miscounted, and as a result, there was quite a bit of confusion about who actually won the presidential election. But there have been other complications as well.

The Democratic Party in Florida encountered problems having Floridians' votes gathered and counted. In 2007, the Democratic Party moved its primary elections ahead of February 5, 2008. This goes against party rules. As a result, Florida's Democrats voted, but their votes were not carried to the Democratic National Convention by a delegate. This added to the frustration that many Floridians have been feeling about the voting process.

The upside to all this confusion is that it led to a renewed passion for voting among citizens, as well as some developments in voting practice and technology. It's leading to a better system for all of us!

On Election Day, November 11, 2000, officials in West Palm Beach, Florida, examine a ballot with a confusing "hanging chad," or partially punched ballot.

Legislative Branch

The executive branch enforces the law, but the legislative branch makes the laws. This branch is made up of a forty-member Senate and a 120-member House of Representatives. These groups are made up of politicians from all over the state. They meet to vote on laws that govern the life of the state. The legislative branch keeps very busy making sure that the laws of Florida are running smoothly.

Not only does the legislative branch enforce laws, but the people who make up this branch also have a duty to speak for you if you are a resident of Florida. They are bound to represent the people who voted for them and elected them into office.

Judicial Branch

The judicial branch is less about enforcing laws and more about interpreting them. The state of Florida has county courts to deal with everyday legal issues and smaller criminal issues, circuit courts for larger cases, and district courts of appeal to settle cases that need more attention than the circuit court can provide. The Florida Supreme Court

The judicial branch of Florida's state government carries out its work in the Federal Courthouse.

Voters line up to take advantage of early voting in 2008. Early voting is one of the many ways that Florida is improving its electoral system.

rules on larger cases, such as those involving the death penalty, as well as any challenges to state or federal law.

Citizenship

There was a time in Florida's history when women and people of color were not allowed to vote. They were prohibited by law or by expensive fees for voting. This meant they had no voice in state government. Today, however, all adult U.S. citizens living in Florida who have not been convicted of a felony are allowed and expected to vote. However, not all of them do. This is the case in every state, but it is changing. People are rediscovering their precious right to vote, and they fervently protect it, especially in Florida.

THE ECONOMY OF FLORIDA

The Industrial Revolution wasn't a war. It was a way of living, working, and seeing the world. While agriculture and localized trade would continue to be booming businesses in Florida (the state generates the most farm income in the Southeast), new opportunities were on the horizon.

Family farms had been the sustaining force in Florida, but large-scale commercial farming and cattle ranching became big business and the order of the day. While other American states were growing tobacco, immigrants brought their rich tradition of tobacco preparation and cigar production with them to Florida, where it could grow into a flourishing industry.

Land for farming wasn't the only desirable natural resource. Prior to World War I, sponge harvesting, citrus crops, and railroad construction made up a large part of Florida's economy. Tourism was another growing business in Florida. As railroads were built and travel became easier, people flocked to Florida to enjoy the sun, beaches, and amazing scenery. This brought money to the people of the state. Today, tourism brings in $57 billion a year to Florida.

Railroads had a huge impact on the growing state. They did much more than ship citrus fruit out and tourists in; they connected the peninsula to the rest of the country.

The Orange Blossom Special, which had its debut in 1921, was one of the many trains that helped people and businesses from all over the country get to the Sunshine State.

As the end of the nineteenth century drew near, so did the age of possibility for the Sunshine State. The land was developed. With the tourists came their spending money. Land in Florida became very desirable and thus quite expensive. This went on for many years, until the Great Depression.

During the Great Depression

Much of Florida's economic boom in the beginning of the twentieth century was rooted in real estate. Real estate requires the giving and

The Great Depression brought hard times to many of Florida's families. Farms were failing. Many families were forced to leave the state in hopes of finding work elsewhere.

taking out of loans, or credit. In 1926, the economic troubles that were soon to wreak havoc on the rest of the country began in Florida. The banking and credit systems fell apart. People could not pay their bills. Many of them lost everything.

Mother Nature was not kind to Florida, either. Dangerous hurricanes washed over the state during these years, destroying property, farms,

Florida and Cuba

In 1898, soldiers came through Tampa, Florida, on their way to fight the Spanish-American War. During this time, many soldiers got to know the Cubans, who wanted to be free of Spanish colonial rule. It's a relationship that lasts today.

During the Spanish-American War, Floridians helped the people living in Cuba fight against tyrannical rule and seek a life where they enjoyed freedom. That war is long over, but Floridians are still supportive of Cubans seeking a life of liberty. Today, the living conditions in Cuba are politically oppressive. Many Cubans flee to Florida, where they can live in a democracy.

and other developments. In 1929, the stock market crashed, bringing ruin to many Americans, including those in Florida.

After World War II

Despite these problems, Florida soon had a big role to play in World War II. Florida's climate made it a perfect place to train soldiers before they went overseas to fight. Transporting soldiers into Florida and training them for their military missions became big business. By the time the war was over, Florida's transportation system was completely up to date and ready for anyone who wanted to do business, or have a great vacation, in the state. The country was recovering from the Great Depression, and Florida was sharing in the boom. Construction, plastics, and international banking came to Florida. With them came jobs and people. With people came even more businesses. Growth snowballed, and soon there were universities

Ten thousand visitors paid $4.95 to enter the Magic Kingdom at Disney World on its first day of business, October 1, 1971. The theme park near Orlando, Florida, still attracts huge crowds.

and exciting new industries, such as the U.S. space program at Cape Canaveral. The space industry makes up $4.5 billion of Florida's economy. Walt Disney World would become a major force in the state's economy as well.

Walt Disney World

Walt Disney World opened in October 1971 after brothers Roy and Walt Disney bought 28,000 acres (11,331 hectares) of land outside Orlando, Florida. In its early stages, it included the Magic Kingdom, a Disney-themed amusement park surrounded by hotels, campgrounds, golfing, and shopping. A monorail train was built to make traveling from lodging to entertainment easy for tourists. It was an amazing success.

In October 1982, Disney World unveiled the EPCOT (Experimental Prototype Community of Tomorrow) Center. It cost more than $1 billion to build and was intended to explore science, discovery, and the potential developments of future societies. The Disney empire continues to expand. Disney is beloved internationally, and it now has amusement parks around the world.

Chapter 5

PEOPLE FROM FLORIDA: PAST AND PRESENT

Florida has a unique ecosystem and an interesting history. However, if you really want to get to know a state, you have to know about more than its beautiful beaches and scenery. You have to know about its people. Florida's welcoming climate has drawn people from all over the world who want to call the state home.

Henry Flagler (1830–1913) Henry Flagler was instrumental in building the railway system that made it possible for cargo and passengers to travel easily in and out of Florida. He was born in New York and moved to Ohio as a very young person to work for relatives. He did not come from a wealthy family and had to work very hard to build a business of his own. He started working in the family business, a mercantile in Ohio. He saved enough money to buy into the business and went on to own businesses in such industries as grain distillery, oil, and hotels. He eventually discovered the business that would make him famous: railroad and town development.

Flagler knew that it would take more than just railroads to make travel possible in Florida. It would take towns with running water, electricity, and sewers to make a civilized path. Flagler had the money to make those things happen, and he did, all over Florida. He and the people who worked for his companies were responsible for opening Florida's doors to imports/exports and tourism. Students interested in capitalism, business, and entrepreneurial undertakings might find Flagler an inspiring role model.

Winslow Homer (1836–1910) Winslow Homer contributed much to the culture of the state of Florida, and indeed, the country. He spent his early years in Boston and worked as an illustrator for *Harper's*

Henry Flagler was a prominent Florida businessman who built railroads and other necessities of community growth across the state.

Weekly. While he worked as an illustrator for many years, his real love, and his best-known works, were his paintings. Many of Homer's paintings were of scenes from the Civil War. This was a time before photographs were practical or plentiful. Sketches, drawings, and paintings of famous battles and Civil War events were how many people learned to picture, imagine, and understand famous events.

"Surf, Prouts Neck" was painted by Winslow Homer in Prouts Neck, Maine. His fascination with the sea is likely part of what inspired his move to Florida later in life.

In addition to Civil War paintings, Homer created many that depicted the beauty of the subtropical land and foliage of Florida and nearby tropical areas. Many of these paintings were of the oceans, boats, and creatures in the area. From his paintings, many people learned of the beauty of the area and made efforts to visit it themselves.

Ernest Hemmingway (1899–1961) Ernest Hemmingway was not born in Florida, but he made it his home. This famous writer was born in Chicago. He traveled to Europe as an American Red Cross ambulance driver during World War I, and he stayed on in Paris, France, as a reporter for some time after that. Soon after, he made Key West, Florida, his home. He loved it because to him it was like being in a foreign country without leaving the United States. It was there that he wrote some of his most famous novels.

Many of his books describe wars—their effects on the people who fight them and the world in which they're fought. He is probably best known for his book *The Old Man and the Sea*, a novel about an elderly Cuban fisherman who catches an exceptionally large fish. For this novel he won the Pulitzer Prize in Fiction and the Nobel Prize for Literature.

Here, Ernest Hemingway is visiting a Cuban fishing town much like the ones that he described in his award-winning books.

James Weldon Johnson (1871–1938) James Weldon Johnson was born in Jacksonville, Florida, to a very humble

Population

You'll need to know more about the people of Florida than the fact that some of them led very interesting lives. You should also know a few things about the people of Florida as a group. There are more people in Florida now than ever before. The population is growing. This is partially because people are moving into Florida from other countries and other states, and partially because the people who live there are living longer.

The population is growing by a rate of 23.5 percent. In 1980, there were 9,746,926 people living in Florida. In 1990, there were 12,937,926. In 2000, there were 15,982,378. A growing population means more energy and economic activity are needed, and that Florida's resources must stretch further than before.

family, but he grew to be a very accomplished and inspiring man. As an African American born before the Civil Rights Movement in the 1960s, his options in life were seen by many people as being limited. But they would certainly have underestimated this amazing man.

Johnson's mother was a schoolteacher and worked tirelessly on behalf of her son's education. She must have felt very proud when he went to college in Atlanta, and then on to study law while working as principal of the Stanton Elementary School. For a year, he ran the first African American newspaper in the United States. It was a short-lived venture, but a historic one.

In 1900, he wrote a poem that has gone on to mean very much to people all over this country. His brother, John Rosamond Johnson, set it to music. It is called "Lift Every Voice and Sing," and it is an anthem for African Americans to this day. The brothers wrote many songs. Some were sung on Broadway or in vaudeville theaters, but it is this song, perhaps, that has the strongest legacy.

Johnson went on to serve as ambassador to Venezuela, Nicaragua, and the Azores. While in the Azores, he wrote a well-known novel, *The Autobiography of an Ex-Colored Man*. He was an important part of the Harlem Renaissance and served as national organizer for the NAACP, the National Association for the Advancement of Colored People.

His life and work spoke to the possibility that African Americans could succeed in contemporary culture and still hold close the rich tradition of their past. This is an ideal we still work toward today.

Marjorie Kinnan Rawlings (1896–1953) Marjorie Kinnan Rawlings was a reporter in the 1920s. This was unusual in a time when many women did not work outside the home. She wrote for newspapers and magazines until 1928, at which time she moved to Florida, where she could grow oranges and write fiction. Her most famous work is *The Yearling*, a novel about a young boy who adopts an orphaned fawn. This tale won a Pulitzer Prize for Fiction and is still famous today as a classic film. She is so beloved as a writer and is such an important part of Florida's culture that her home has been preserved as it was when she lived there.

Janet Reno, a native of Dade County, Florida, was the first woman appointed attorney general of the United States. In this photo, she is being applauded by President Bill Clinton.

Janet Reno (1938–) Janet Reno was born in Florida and received her early education in Dade County. She went to Coral Gables High School before leaving for college in Ithaca, New York. She went on to Harvard Law School but had a hard time finding work as an attorney in a culture that didn't yet welcome the idea of women practicing law.

However, Reno did practice law—and very successfully, too. In 1971, she became director of the Judiciary Committee of the Florida House of Representatives. Two years later, she accepted a position with the Dade County State Attorney's

Office. She left five years later to practice law in a private firm, but it wasn't long before she was elected state attorney general for Dade County. This was a big step for women in law, and a huge step for her personally.

Reno was elected four more times in Dade County and practiced for many years before she was appointed Attorney General of the United States by President Bill Clinton in 1993, and then again in 1997. She is an example to women in law and is a powerful influence on our current legal system.

Norman Thagard (1943–) Norman Thagard calls Jacksonville, Florida, home. He went to grade school in Florida, graduated from Paxon Senior High School, and then went on to Florida State University to earn a bachelor's—and then a master's—degree in engineering. He became a doctor of medicine at the University of Texas Southwestern Medical School and later earned a master's in business administration from the University of Florida.

Certainly, Thagard's vast education is interesting, but he is most famous for his career with the National Aeronautics and Space Administration (NASA). He became an astronaut candidate in January 1978. He's been on five space flights and has spent more than 140 days in outer space. He's been a crew member on both American and Russian flights, which is something that would have been unthinkable in his early career when U.S.–Russian relations were poor.

Jim Morrison (1943–1971) Rock icon Jim Morrison was a Florida native. Born in Melbourne, Florida, he spent many early years in Clearwater and attended classes at both St. Petersburg Junior College and Florida State University.

Morrison lived there until 1964, when he moved to Los Angeles, California, to study film at the University of California, Los Angeles (UCLA). A year later, he and a fellow UCLA student, Ray Manzarek, teamed up with drummer John Densmore and guitarist Robby Krieger to form the band we now know as the Doors.

Perhaps the best-known psychedelic rock band of their time, the Doors' biggest hits include songs like "Light My Fire," "Gloria," "Hello, I Love You," and "People Are Strange." Morrison died young in Paris in 1971. He has become a source of much myth, mystery, and legend. His Parisian grave is a pilgrimage spot for people who are interested in rock and roll, the bohemian lifestyle, and popular culture.

Timeline

1492–1700	Explorers and travelers from Europe come to the land we now know as Florida.
1878–1897	Tourism begins to evolve as a major draw to Florida.
1914–1918	Soldiers leave to fight World War I; a certain amount of military training is done in Florida.
1920s	Floridian industry enjoys a growth spurt.
1929–1941	Florida, and the rest of the nation, suffers during the Great Depression.
1926	The Great Miami Hurricane hits Florida, killing hundreds of people.
1935	The Florida Park System is established to help protect natural and recreational sites.
1941	World War II brings soldiers in training to Florida; military training becomes a major industry in Florida.
1950	Frozen orange juice concentrate is invented; Florida's economy gets a huge boost.
1961	Astronauts blast off from Cape Canaveral in Florida, which would become the starting point of the first mission to the moon.
1965	Walt Disney announces plans to build Walt Disney World in Orlando.
1977	A freeze causes significant loss to citrus farmers.
1993	Janet Reno is named Attorney General of the United States by President Clinton.
2000	In the presidential election, the voting results are unclear, resulting in an election recount. The decision eventually goes to the U.S. Supreme Court, with George W. Bush ultimately receiving the majority of electoral votes over Al Gore.
2004	Florida is hit by four major hurricanes: Charley, Frances, Ivan, and Jeanne. Damages cost the state's economy $42 billion.
2008	Though the nation experiences a devastating number of home foreclosures, Florida has the highest mortgage delinquency rate in the country.

Florida at a Glance

State motto	"In God We Trust"
State capital	Tallahassee
State flower	Orange blossom
State bird	Mockingbird
State tree	Cabbage palmetto
Year of statehood	March 3, 1845 (twenty-seventh state)
State nickname	Sunshine State
Total area	65,758 square miles (170,312 sq km); twenty-second in size
Approximate population at most recent census	15,982,378
Length of coastline	1,197 miles (1,926.38 km)
Highest elevation	Britton Hills, at 345 feet (105 meters)
Lowest elevation	sea level, where Florida meets the Atlantic Ocean and the Gulf of Mexico
Major rivers	St. Johns River, St. Marys River, Suwannee River

State Flag

State Seal

Major lakes	Lake Okeechobee, Lake George
Hottest temperature recorded	109 degrees Fahrenheit (43 degrees Celsius), on June 29, 1931, in Monticello
Coldest temperature recorded	–2°F (–19°C), on February 13, 1899, in Tallahassee
Origin of state name	Spanish word for "feast of flowers"
Chief agricultural products	Citrus fruits
Major industries	Tourism, agriculture, electronics

State Bird

State Flower

GLOSSARY

chad A piece of paper punched out of a paper ballot (like a hole punch) to indicate a voter's vote.

colonization The act of sending explorers and settlers to exert political control over a foreign piece of land.

ecosystem The plants and animals living and functioning together in a certain natural environment.

Great Depression A period in the 1930s when the American economy failed and people experienced widespread poverty and homelessness.

Industrial Revolution A period during the late eighteenth century and early nineteenth century when people turned from farming and craftsmanship to factories and machine-supported businesses.

mercantile A general store that carried clothing, hardware, groceries, and anything else needed for daily life.

Parisian From or in Paris, France.

peninsula A landmass surrounded on three sides by water.

population The number and types of people living in a certain area.

subtropical Refers to regions bordering tropical areas.

tropical Refers to areas, and the plants and animals found there, within a certain range of the earth's equator.

FOR MORE INFORMATION

Division of Historical Resources

Office of Cultural and Historical Programs

500 S. Bronough Street

Tallahassee, FL 32399-0250

(850) 245-6300

Web site: http://www.flheritage.com/kids

This government agency is dedicated to preserving and sharing the cultural history of Florida. Its informative and fun Web site is tailored for young people.

Everglades National Park

40001 State Road 9336

Homestead, FL 33034-6733

(305) 242-7700

Web site: http://www.nps.gov/ever

This is the official contact information for Everglades National Park. If you're looking for information on this one-of-a-kind ecosystem, this is a great place to start learning.

Florida Festivals and Events Association, Inc. (FFEA)

4174 Palo Verde Drive

Boynton Beach, FL 33436

(561) 736-7071

Web site: http://www.ffea.com

The Florida Festivals and Events Association, Inc. (FFEA) is an organization that supports, organizes, and publicizes special events in Florida. If you're interested in tourism or local celebrations, this organization could be helpful to you. It offers volunteer and internship opportunities.

University of Florida: Florida History Online

P.O. Box 117007

Gainesville, FL 32611-7001

(352) 273-2774

Web site: http://www.unf.edu/floridahistoryonline/projects/proj-b-p.html

The University of Florida gathers and makes available information about Florida's history for students, teachers, and anyone else interested. Information online includes discussions of Florida's history, ideas and resources for projects, and links to other interesting sites and pieces.

University of Florida's P. K. Yonge Library of Florida History

P.O. Box 117007

Gainesville, FL 32611-7001

(352) 273-2774

Web site: http://www.uflib.ufl.edu/spec/pkyonge/index.html

The University of Florida has a special collection of books, documents, and artifacts that focus on Florida's history. For more information about this collection—or to see select documents online—visit the Web site. Some materials may be available via interlibrary loan.

Web Sites

Due to the changing nature of Internet links, Rosen Publishing has developed an online list of Web sites related to the subject of this book. This site is updated regularly. Please use this link to access the list:

http://www.rosenlinks.com/uspp/flpp

FOR FURTHER READING

Barnes, Jay. *Florida's Hurricane History*. Chapel Hill, NC: University of North Carolina Press, 2007.

Barnett, Cynthia. *Mirage: Florida and the Vanishing Water of the Eastern U.S.* Ann Arbor, MI: University of Michigan Press, 2004.

Colburn, David R. *From Yellow Dog Democrats to Red State Republicans: Florida and its Politics since 1940*. Gainesville, FL: University Press of Florida, 2007.

Foglesong, Richard. *Married to the Mouse: Walt Disney World and Orlando*. New Haven, CT: Yale University Press, 2001.

Grunwald, Michael. *The Swamp: the Everglades, Florida and the Politics of Paradise*. New York, NY: Simon & Schuster, 2006.

Levin, Ted. *Liquid Land: A Journey Through the Florida Everglades*. Athens, GA: University of Georgia Press, 2003

Lynch, Wayne. *The Everglades*. Lanham, MD: National Book Network, 2007.

McNally, David. *Florida*. Mankato, MN: Coughlan Publishing, 2003.

Waitley, Douglas. *Easygoing Guide to Natural Florida*. Sarasota, FL: Pineapple Press, 2008.

Weitzel, Kelly G. *Journeys with Florida's Indians*. Gainesville, FL: University Press of Florida, 2002.

BIBLIOGRAPHY

Derr, Mark. "Network of Waterways Traced to Ancient Florida Culture." *New York Times*, July 23, 2002. Retrieved December 2, 2008 (http://query.nytimes.com/gst/fullpage. html?res=9E03E6DF1438F930A15754C0A9649C8B63).

Division of Historical Resources, Florida Department of State. "Archeology." Retrieved December 2, 2008 (http://www.flheritage.com/archaeology).

Division of Historical Resources, Florida Department of State. "Florida Facts and History." Retrieved December 2, 2008 (http://www.flheritage.com/facts).

Florida Department of Health. "Florida's Safe Beaches." Retrieved December 2, 2008 (http://www.doh.state.fl.us/Environment/community/aquatic/beach_index_ indepth.html).

Milanich, Jerald T. "Florida's Indians from Ancient Times to the Present." 1998. Retrieved December 2, 2008 (http://www.flmnh.ufl.edu/vertpaleo/aucilla11_1/ milanich.htm).

Moreno, Dario. "Exile Political Power: Cubans in the United States Political System." Florida International University. Retrieved December 2, 2008 (http:// 64.233.169.132/search?q=cache:jXkXLMg-k0cJ:metropolitan.fiu.edu/downloads/ exile percent2520political percent2520power.doc+cubans+in+the+united+states+ political+system+dario&hl=en&ct=clnk&cd=1&gl=us&client=safari).

MSNBC. "Clinton Gets Most Democratic Votes in Fla." January 29, 2008. Retrieved December 12, 2008 (http://www.msnbc.msn.com/id/22904383).

MyFlorida.com. "Government." Retrieved December 2, 2008 (http://www.myflorida.com/ taxonomy/government).

Natural Resources Defense Council. "Issues: Global Warming." October 23, 2008. Retrieved December 2, 2008 (http://www.nrdc.org/globalWarming/nflorida.asp).

Seminole Tribe of Florida. "History: Where We Came From." Retrieved December 2, 2008 (http://www.seminoletribe.com/history).

StateofFlorida.com. "Florida Quick Facts." Retrieved December 2, 2008 (http://www. stateofflorida.com/Portal/DesktopDefault.aspx?tabid=95).

About the Author

Sarah Sawyer is a culture and lifestyle writer living in Minneapolis, Minnesota. She has been to Florida many times over the last twenty-five years to spend time with relatives who are longtime residents.

Photo Credits

Cover (top left) © Les Snider/Photo Images/Corbis; cover (top right) © Robert Sullivan/AFP/Getty Images; cover (bottom) Don Emmert/AFP/Getty Images; pp. 3, 6, 12, 21, 24, 30, 39, 40 (right), 41 (both) Wikipedia; p. 4 (top) © GeoAtlas; p. 7 © Stephen Frink/Aurora Photos/Corbis; pp. 8, 16 Courtesy of the University of Texas Libraries, The University of Texas at Austin; p. 9 © Nik Wheeler/Corbis; p. 11 © www.istockphoto.com/Greg Cooksey; p. 13 © Hulton Archive/Getty Images; pp. 14, 25, 31 © Granger Collection; p. 19 © Courtesy of the Office of the Governor of Florida; p. 20 © Bruce Weaver/Getty Images; p. 22 © Gary I. Rothstein/Corbis; p. 26 © MPI/Getty Images; p. 28 © Yael Joel/Time & Life Pictures/Getty Images; p. 32 © Yale University Art Gallery/Art Resource, NY; p. 33 © Alfred Eisenstaedt/Pix/Time & Life Pictures/Getty Images; p. 36 © Stephen Boitano/Sygma/Corbis; p. 40 (left) Courtesy of Robesus, Inc.

Designer: Les Kanturek; Editor: Nicholas Croce;
Photo Researcher: Marty Levick